ALSO BY ED SLOTT

Stay Rich for Life!

Your Complete Retirement Planning Road Map

The Retirement Savings Time Bomb . . . and How to Defuse It

Parlay Your IRA into a Family Fortune

STAY RICH FOR LIFE! WORKBOOK

STAY RICH FOR LIFE! WORKBOOK

Growing & Protecting Your Money in Turbulent Times

Ed Slott

BALLANTINE BOOKS

NEW YORK

A Ballantine Books Trade Paperback Original

Published in the United States by Ballantine Books,
an imprint of The Random House Publishing Group,
a division of Random House, Inc., New York.

BALLANTINE and colophon are registered trademarks of
Random House, Inc.

ISBN 978-0-345-51443-1

Printed in the United States of America

www.ballantinebooks.com

8 9 7

Book design by Mary A. Wirth

A Cautionary Note to Readers of the
Stay Rich for Life! Workbook:

"Stay Rich for Life" is a commonsense approach to personal finance. In practical advice books, as in life, there are no guarantees, and readers are cautioned to rely on their own judgment about their individual circumstances and to act accordingly. Readers are also reminded that the approach described here is intended for informational purposes only and is not meant to take the place of professional advice. The laws in this area are complex and constantly changing. You should consult with an experienced professional to apply the relevant laws in your state to your unique situation.

In addition, I do not endorse, sell, or advise on investments or any financial products such as life insurance, annuities, mutual funds, stocks, bonds, or similar products and I have limited knowledge of these financial products. I am also not a partner or an owner of any company that sells or advises on investment products like the ones mentioned in the above sentence.

—ED SLOTT

A Cautionary Note Regarding Members of Ed Slott's Elite IRA Advisor Group™ and Ed Slott's Master Elite Advisor Group:

I have educated and trained these advisors on tax and estate planning, but I do not train them on financial products or investments. I am a tax advisor and not an investment advisor. I do not endorse any of the financial products or investments they sell or advise on. I do not sell these products and have limited financial product knowledge. I do not partner with any of these advisors, nor do I earn any income from sales of their products or services. They do pay our company an annual fee for the advanced education and training they receive year-round.

I am not responsible for investments or financial products or services you may purchase from any of these advisors. You should check all of their credentials.

—ED SLOTT

Contents

STAY RICH FOR LIFE! WORKBOOK

Let's Get Started!

How This Workbook Is Organized

First, I recommend that you read *Stay Rich for Life!* by Ed Slott. There, I introduce you to my five-step system for taking control of saving, growing, and keeping your money:

1. **Know who you are and where you are.**
2. **Educate yourself.**
3. **Avoid mistakes.**
4. **Don't be shortsighted.**
5. **Take action in small, consistent steps.**
   (Pay particular attention to this one, as small, consistent steps result in big victories!)

This workbook can be used independently of that book, but it is a more powerful tool when used in conjunction with it. The workbook is organized in exactly the order you should use it.

How to Use This Workbook

Use the *Stay Rich for Life! Workbook* to catalog all the data you will gather and all the actions you have taken or will be taking to implement your personal "Stay Rich for Life" wealth accumulation and distribution protection plan. There is a ton of information here, but just take it bit by bit and you will be amazed at the progress you will make.

The information you enter is always subject to alteration based on changes in the tax laws, changes in the financial markets, changes in your life and family situation, and any other changes you want to make along the way to reflect your current feelings, needs, or wishes.

Because of the inevitability of change, this workbook really becomes a living document that grows with you. If you keep it up to date, it will not only benefit you, but will become an invaluable resource to your loved ones for decades to come.

Take your time and be thorough. It's a big job that could take a few weeks, which is okay. The idea is to gather enough information to create a long-term wealth accumulation and retirement distribution plan for your financial security. This workbook is the foundation you need to get started.

From there, your task is much easier. Simply update and revise the sections affected by changes in data. Using this procedure, you will always have the most current plan, based on up-to-date personal and financial information. This workbook really can be worth a fortune to you and to those you care about.

The Benefits to You

Three words: **Peace of Mind!**

I have created both the "Stay Rich for Life" system and the *Stay Rich for Life! Workbook* to:

- Make it easy for you to achieve immediate and lifelong financial security for you and your family

- Make it easy (and maybe even fun!) for you to jump right in and get started

- Make it so easy that you start to see benefits right away

- Make it so usable you will keep using it and updating it as major events change in your life or the lives of your loved ones

- Make sure that you receive benefits right now and throughout your retirement years, and then have this program benefit your loved ones for decades more

- Make it easy to be able to share this information with your professional advisors, such as your financial planner, attorney, and tax professional

- Make sure that . . .

  1. You are working with the most knowledgeable professional advisors

  2. Your professional advisors are better able to help you and your family

Warning!!
What You WON'T Get from This System

"Stay Rich for Life" is *not* . . .

• **A get-rich-quick scheme or overnight success program.**

This will take you some time at the beginning as you start to work through it. Once you have most of the information and planning set up, then it will require only a minimal amount of time to maintain the plan and make required changes as key events in your life and the lives of your loved ones change.

• **Something you should do without the advice of knowledgeable and capable professional advisors.**

But you do need to be educated about the process, and that is what you are learning here.

First, Just Relax and Read Stay Rich for Life! *by Ed Slott*

As you are reading, make notes to yourself. Write down items that you might want to know more about.

Don't worry about any items that you may not understand. There's no need to dig in yet.

You should go through the planning process first, and at the end of the workbook, you'll find that you will have a keen sense of the importance of this information to you.

ITEMS I WANT TO KNOW MORE ABOUT:

_____

_____

_____

_____

_____

_____

_____

Part I

THE FINANCIAL STORM

YOU'RE ON YOUR OWN TO SECURE YOUR FINANCIAL FUTURE

I have left some space after each of these items for you to jot down your own thoughts or action to take.

• **We are entering the Y.O.Y.O. economy.** You're on your own. The government cannot help you. Your company or employer cannot help you, either. They are out of money. You are on your own, and only you can help yourself.

• **Take control of your own money.** You need to start saving and building your nest egg *now* to secure your own future—the more time you have, the more you can accumulate. And since you don't really know what the eventual tax on your tax-deferred wealth accumulation (contributions plus earnings) will be when you or your loved ones start withdrawing the money, you need a nest egg protection plan, too.

• **The tax collector has a plan. . . . Do you?** Our tax system is a penalty on savers. You must approach any savings and investment plan for retirement with the assumption that Congress will find a way to highly tax your tax-deferred accumulations. Taxes will increase in the coming years due to a combination of looming financial crises I call S.H.I.P., which stands for:

Social Security

Health care

Income taxes

Pensions

You will need to prepare for when that S.H.I.P. hits the fan later on!

Also, you have to create your plan with the help of professional advisors who have specialized training.

• **It's how much you keep (after taxes) that counts.** Retirement accounts are heavily taxed, both for estate tax and income tax, not to mention the state versions of these taxes and post-death expenses that will be a burden to your loved ones. You need to develop an *"exit strategy"* as well, which is a distribution plan so that you do not end up with the government plan.

The government plan means paying the highest taxes and paying them sooner than you have to.

Your plan means minimizing taxes at retirement and forever.

ITEMS I WANT TO KNOW MORE ABOUT:

_____

_____

_____

_____

PROBLEM AREAS:

_____

_____

_____

_____

ACTION I SHOULD TAKE:

_____

_____

_____

_____

_____

CHOOSING (FINANCIAL, LEGAL, TAX) ADVISORS—KEY QUESTIONS TO ASK ADVISORS

Make sure your advisor has the specialized knowledge necessary to help you create and implement your investment and retirement savings plan. How will you know? Ask the following key questions:

1. "I know this area requires specialized knowledge in investment and wealth accumulation plus retirement distribution planning. Do you have expertise in these areas? How would I know that?"

NOTES:

_____

_____

_____

_____

2. "What books have you read on these topics?" (Look at the books. If they crack when you open them . . . run. They've never been read!)

NOTES:

_____

_____

_____

_____

_____

_____

_____

_____

_____

3. "What professional training do you take in investment and retirement planning? What courses or programs have you taken? Can you show me the last course manual you received?"

NOTES:

_____

_____

_____

_____

_____

_____

_____

_____

_____

4. "How do you stay current on key investment products and tools and new retirement plan tax and distribution rules? What services or resources do you rely on to stay up to date? Can you show me a sample?"

NOTES:

_____

_____

_____

_____

_____

_____

_____

_____

5. "What are my best investment choices? How do you determine the best options for me?"

NOTES:

_____

_____

_____

_____

_____

_____

_____

_____

_____

_____

6. "How do you take the tax consequences into account for my investments? What is the latest savings plan distribution tax rule you are aware of? When did that occur?"

NOTES:

_____

_____

_____

_____

_____

_____

_____

_____

_____

7. "How would you keep track of my investments? What are all my distribution plan choices? How do you determine the best option for me?"

NOTES:

_____

_____

_____

_____

_____

_____

_____

_____

_____

_____

8. "What are the key events that would trigger a need to review my total financial picture (divorce, children, loss of job, death, retirement, inheritance, etc.)?"

NOTES:

_____

_____

_____

_____

_____

_____

_____

_____

_____

Here are a few especially challenging questions to ask potential advisors that will show whether they really know their stuff.

9. "Can you show me the IRS life expectancy tables?"

NOTES:

_____

_____

_____

_____

_____

_____

_____

_____

_____

10. "How will you make sure that my beneficiaries will get the 'stretch' option?"

NOTES:

_____

_____

_____

_____

_____

_____

_____

_____

_____

_____

11. "Who do *you* turn to when you have questions on financial, legal, or tax matters?" (No one can know it all.)

NOTES:

_____

_____

_____

_____

_____

_____

_____

_____

_____

_____

_____

12. "Do you have someone in place to implement my wealth accumulation and retirement distribution plan if something happens to you? Who is it, and what are his or her credentials?"

NOTES:

_____

_____

_____

_____

_____

_____

_____

_____

_____

_____

FINDING AN EXPERT ADVISOR

I hear stories all the time from consumers who have reached what I call the "crossover point," meaning that they realize they know more than their advisor, and they want to move to an advisor who knows more than they do.

You don't want to fool around here. You want competent advisors to do your planning.

In reaction to this growing consumer demand, our website, www.irahelp.com, has a section where consumers just like you can click in and find advisors with advanced knowledge in exactly this type of planning. These advisors are members of a group I created called "Ed Slott's Elite IRA Advisor Group,™" and I list their names and contact information on our website.

My mission is to provide you with access to highly trained advisors who have specialized knowledge in both the first half *and,* especially, the winning (distribution planning) half of the wealth accumulation and protection game. Many consumers are under-served in the latter half by the average financial advisor who lacks this key knowledge. As a consumer who may have spent a lifetime building your retirement savings, you deserve to move up to an advisor who can help you keep more of what you have saved from the government and pass more of it on to your loved ones in the most tax-favored way.

Ed Slott's Elite IRA Advisor Group™ and Ed Slott's Master Elite IRA Advisor Group

HOW ARE ADVISORS CHOSEN TO BE LISTED ON OUR WEBSITE?

We list only those advisors *who continue their training* as members of our Elite IRA Advisor Group. We will not maintain on our list an advisor who has taken some training but not continued with his or her education in this highly specialized and complex area. Tax laws and IRS rulings are constantly being released and changed, and we want consumers to know that all advisors listed on our site are continuing their education and, at a minimum, being exposed to these developments so that the advice they give you is based on current tax rules.

To be a member of Ed Slott's Elite IRA Advisor Group, advisors must first go through our basic training program. For most of our members, this means that they have either attended our intense two-day IRA training program (Instant IRA Success) or have taken one of the (similar) programs we provide to individual companies.

WHAT IS THE DIFFERENCE BETWEEN AN ELITE IRA ADVISOR AND A *MASTER* ELITE IRA ADVISOR?

They are both members of Ed Slott's Elite IRA Advisor Group, so they are both in our continuing advanced education programs.

After advisors have been in our Elite IRA Advisor program for two years, they can then advance to our *Master* Elite IRA Advisor program.

The Master Elite IRA Advisor is our highest level of advanced education in IRA and retirement tax planning. These advisors have had both our basic training and a minimum of two years with us on top of that, and are committed to continuing that training.

To obtain the most current information on these financial advisors, go to www.irahelp.com. Then click on the area that says "Looking for an advisor who knows IRAs?"

The advisors who are listed are not only well versed in all aspects of the first half of the game (wealth accumulation), but have been personally trained by me or a member of my team in the exit strategy (distribution planning)—the winning half of the game.

Nevertheless, be sure to ask any of these advisors the same key questions listed in the preceding section. No advisor, even one I may have trained, is exempt from your thorough examination. Your first loyalty is to yourself and your family. As already noted, to remain a member of this group and continue to be listed on our website, these advisors have to meet certain education, testing, and attendance requirements. In this area, there are no promises or guarantees. Any advisor you are considering, including advisors listed on our site, must therefore be fully checked out by *you*.

Part II

THE FIRST HALF OF THE GAME

YOUR SAVINGS AND WEALTH ACCUMULATION PLAN

I have left some space after each of the items in this section for you to jot down your own thoughts or action to take.

• **More, more, more!** When you become an instant saver and create your own wealth-building plan, you will have *more* money for you now, *more* for your retirement, *more* for your loved ones . . . and more of it tax free!

• **Save automatically.** Force the discipline of saving into becoming a habit by participating in your local 529 college savings plan, a traditional 401(k), 403(b), or 457, or a Roth 401(k) and Roth 403(b) plan at work, a Keogh or SEP IRA plan if you're self-employed, or an individual retirement account (IRA and Roth IRA)—and put your money to work for you.

• **Put time on your side.** Portfolios can weather more financial storms during the accumulation phase of building wealth (growth investing)—because of time and the power of compounding—than they can during the distribution phase in retirement, where there is less time to recoup losses.

• **Plan for the long term.** It takes time to put together a solid, wealth-building portfolio of well-allocated assets, and especially in a down market, stocks are not always the place to be—sometimes cash is king.

Think Through What Your Goals Are

DO YOU NEED TO FINANCE COLLEGE EDUCATION?

_____

_____

_____

_____

ARE THERE LONG-TERM MEDICAL COSTS THAT NEED TO BE COVERED?

_____

_____

_____

_____

ARE YOU HOPING TO BUY A SECOND HOME?

_____

_____

_____

_____

DO YOU NEED A NEW CAR THIS YEAR OR IN FIVE YEARS?

_____

_____

_____

_____

WHEN WOULD YOU LIKE TO RETIRE?

_____

_____

_____

_____

You need to think through all of these short- and long-term goals as you plan for the future.

• **Tax-free withdrawals.** Nothing is better than tax-free planning, so keep that in mind. Do you have a flexible spending plan at your job that allows you to put money aside, tax free, for medical and dependent care costs? Remember the Roth IRA: While taxes are paid up front on contributions, savings and interest grow tax free forever for withdrawal.

• **Never run out of money.** Investing in annuities can solve worries about running out of money in retirement because they guarantee an income for life.

ITEMS I WANT TO KNOW MORE ABOUT:

_____

_____

_____

_____

_____

_____

PROBLEM AREAS:

_____

_____

_____

_____

_____

_____

ACTION I SHOULD TAKE:

_____

_____

_____

_____

_____

_____

GATHERING YOUR FINANCIAL INFORMATION

Before your financial advisor can help you create a plan, you must know what you have, who owns it (solely yours or owned jointly), where the assets are, and what your net worth is.

Take an Inventory of All Your Assets

Make a list of your property and the current value of each item.

If space does not permit here, then use a separate page to enter this information. You may also enter it on your computer so it will be easy to update with current values. This is a guide to remind you to include this property.

CASH AND CERTIFICATES OF DEPOSITS (NOT IN IRAS)

_____

_____

_____

_____

_____

STOCKS, BONDS, FUNDS (NOT IN IRAS)

_____

_____

_____

_____

_____

_____

STOCK OPTIONS

_____

_____

_____

_____

TREASURY BONDS, NOTES, OR BILLS (NOT IN IRAS)

_____

_____

_____

_____

MUNICIPAL BONDS

_____

_____

_____

_____

LIFE INSURANCE

_____

_____

_____

_____

ANNUITIES (NOT IN IRAS)

_____

_____

_____

_____

RECEIVABLES:

MONEY OWED TO YOU ON LOANS YOU MADE

_____

_____

_____

_____

MONEY OWED TO YOU FROM BUSINESS INTERESTS OR SALES OF PROPERTY

_____

_____

_____

_____

COPYRIGHTS OR PATENTS

_____

_____

_____

_____

HOME

_____

_____

_____

_____

MORTGAGES OR OTHER LOANS OUTSTANDING

_____

_____

_____

_____

OTHER LIABILITIES

_____

_____

_____

_____

VACATION HOME

_____

_____

_____

_____

OTHER HOMES

_____

_____

_____

_____

_____

_____

_____

CONDOS AND CO-OPS

_____

_____

_____

_____

FOREIGN PROPERTY

_____

_____

_____

_____

OTHER REAL ESTATE

_____

_____

_____

_____

_____

_____

_____

_____

COLLECTIBLES, ANTIQUES, JEWELRY, AND OTHER VALUABLES

_____

_____

_____

_____

_____

_____

_____

VALUE OF BUSINESS INTERESTS

_____

_____

_____

_____

FAMILY BUSINESS

_____

_____

_____

_____

AUTOS, BOATS, PLANES

_____

_____

_____

_____

_____

_____

_____

_____

HOUSEHOLD FURNISHINGS

_____

_____

_____

_____

_____

_____

_____

CLUB MEMBERSHIPS

_____

_____

_____

_____

INHERITANCES

_____

_____

_____

_____

_____

_____

FUNDS IN TRUSTS

_____

_____

_____

_____

_____

_____

Retirement Accounts

• *Company Retirement Plans*

401(K)S

_____

_____

_____

_____

_____

ROTH 401(K)S

_____

_____

_____

_____

_____

403(B)S

_____

_____

_____

_____

ROTH 403(B)S

_____

_____

_____

_____

457 PLANS

_____

_____

_____

_____

KEOGH PLANS

_____

_____

_____

_____

_____

_____

• *Other Company Retirement Accounts*

_____

_____

_____

_____

_____

_____

• Your Own IRAs

IRAS

_____

_____

_____

_____

_____

_____

SEP IRAS (SIMPLIFIED EMPLOYEE PENSION IRAS)

_____

_____

_____

_____

_____

_____

SIMPLE IRAS (SAVINGS INCENTIVE MATCH PLANS FOR EMPLOYEES IRAS)

_____

_____

_____

_____

_____

_____

ROTH IRAS

_____

_____

_____

_____

_____

_____

• Inherited Retirement Accounts

These are retirement accounts you inherited from someone else. These must be kept separate from your own retirement accounts.

INHERITED IRAS

_____

_____

_____

_____

INHERITED ROTH IRAS

_____

_____

_____

_____

INHERITED COMPANY RETIREMENT PLANS [401(K)S, 403(B)S, ROTH 401(K)S, ETC.]

_____

_____

_____

_____

Add It All Up

What is the approximate value of your overall worth?

ITEMS I WANT TO KNOW MORE ABOUT:

_____

_____

_____

_____

_____

_____

PROBLEM AREAS:

_____

_____

_____

_____

_____

ACTION I SHOULD TAKE:

_____

_____

_____

_____

_____

_____

GATHERING YOUR PERSONAL INFORMATION

Personal Information

You need to know who all the players in the game will be.

Your Family Tree

Family members and loved ones you want to provide for:

PARENTS OR GRANDPARENTS

_____

_____

_____

_____

_____

_____

OTHER OLDER RELATIVES OR LOVED ONES

_____

_____

_____

_____

SPOUSE

_____

_____

_____

_____

PARTNER

_____

_____

_____

_____

CHILDREN

_____

_____

_____

_____

_____

GRANDCHILDREN

_____

_____

_____

_____

_____

GREAT-GRANDCHILDREN

_____

_____

_____

_____

FRIENDS

_____

_____

_____

_____

_____

_____

_____

OTHER RELATIVES

_____

_____

_____

_____

_____

_____

_____

Charities

_____

_____

_____

_____

Business Partners

_____

_____

_____

_____

OTHERS

_____

_____

_____

_____

_____

_____

_____

_____

Primary Beneficiaries Named on Beneficiary Form

_____

_____

_____

_____

_____

_____

Contingent Beneficiaries Named on Beneficiary Forms

_____

_____

_____

_____

_____

_____

Make notes about your loved ones (those you want to provide for from the preceding list). Include items such as:

Prior marriages

Children of prior marriages

Beneficiaries who might not be good handling a large inheritance

Providing for future grandchildren

Special needs of your intended beneficiaries (e.g., medical or education needs)

Family dynamics (who gets along and who does not)

OTHER ITEMS THAT YOU WANT TO MAKE A NOTE OF

_____

_____

_____

_____

_____

Names and Contact Information for All People Who Will Have Responsibilities for Your Estate

EXECUTORS OR ADMINISTRATORS

_____

_____

_____

_____

_____

TRUSTEES OF TRUSTS

_____

_____

_____

_____

_____

DOCTORS

_____

_____

_____

_____

_____

_____

OTHERS

_____

_____

_____

_____

_____

_____

Names and Contact Information for All Key Financial Advisors

FINANCIAL PLANNER

_____

_____

_____

_____

ATTORNEY

_____

_____

_____

_____

ACCOUNTANT

_____

_____

_____

_____

LIFE INSURANCE PROFESSIONAL

_____

_____

_____

_____

STOCKBROKERS

_____

_____

_____

_____

BANK CONTACTS

_____

_____

_____

_____

CLERGY

_____

_____

_____

_____

_____

OTHERS

_____

_____

_____

_____

_____

LOCATION OF ESSENTIAL PLANNING DOCUMENTS

This lets you and everyone else know where everything is located. This is obviously not for public knowledge. This is for your eyes only and to share with trusted loved ones who will be inheriting from you and will need to know where many of these key documents are located.

Who is the person (or people) you will want to have access to the information in this workbook? This workbook contains essential financial and personal information, and you have made great efforts to keep a written record of it. Make sure your efforts pay off by leaving instructions or a *separate note* ("to be opened upon my becoming disabled or on my death") with your loved ones or advisors about where they can find this workbook when they need it.

This workbook listing can be especially helpful if you become incompetent to handle your own affairs and need the assistance of others. This will help them locate essential documents, such as a power of attorney, which can allow others you trust to make financial and health decisions if you are unable to make them for yourself.

COMPUTER PASSWORDS

Loved ones and advisors will need to access all computer and e-mail records that may contain financial or personal information you want them to have.

_____

_____

_____

_____

_____

_____

_____

_____

_____

These will allow access to your banking and other financial records, as well as your employer-sponsored, personal IRA, or any other retirement account information.

_____

_____

_____

_____

_____

SAFE-DEPOSIT BOXES

_____

_____

_____

_____

Who has access?

_____

_____

_____

_____

Under what name is the box registered?

_____

_____

_____

_____

SAFES OR OTHER PLACES WHERE VALUABLES MAY BE STORED

_____

_____

_____

_____

BIRTH CERTIFICATE

_____

_____

_____

_____

ADOPTION PAPERS

_____

_____

_____

_____

MARRIAGE CERTIFICATES

_____

_____

_____

_____

SOCIAL SECURITY BENEFITS

_____

_____

_____

_____

VETERANS BENEFITS

_____

_____

_____

_____

MILITARY INFORMATION

_____

_____

_____

_____

IMMIGRATION AND NATURALIZATION DOCUMENTS

_____

_____

_____

_____

_____

_____

PASSPORTS

_____

_____

_____

_____

_____

_____

DEATH CERTIFICATES

These should include those of anyone you have inherited property from, so you know when you inherited the property.

_____

_____

_____

_____

_____

WILLS

_____

_____

_____

_____

TRUSTS

_____

_____

_____

_____

PERSONAL TAX RETURNS

_____

_____

_____

_____

BUSINESS TAX RETURNS

_____

_____

_____

_____

BUSINESS OR PARTNERSHIP AGREEMENTS

_____

_____

_____

_____

BUSINESS OR PERSONAL CONTRACTS IN FORCE

_____

_____

_____

_____

GIFT TAX RETURNS

_____

_____

_____

_____

DEEDS TO REAL ESTATE

_____

_____

_____

_____

MORTGAGES

_____

_____

_____

_____

BANK STATEMENTS AND CANCELED CHECKS

_____

_____

_____

_____

FINANCIAL STATEMENTS

_____

_____

_____

_____

LIVING WILLS

_____

_____

_____

_____

HEALTH CARE PROXIES

_____

_____

_____

_____

OTHER MEDICAL DIRECTIVES

_____

_____

_____

_____

_____

_____

FUNERAL INSTRUCTIONS

_____

_____

_____

_____

_____

_____

_____

LIFE AND HEALTH INSURANCE POLICIES

_____

_____

_____

_____

_____

_____

_____

LONG-TERM-CARE POLICIES

_____

_____

_____

_____

POWERS OF ATTORNEY

_____

_____

_____

_____

CEMETERY PLOTS

_____

_____

_____

_____

DIVORCE OR SEPARATION AGREEMENTS

_____

_____

_____

_____

PRENUPTIAL AGREEMENTS

_____

_____

_____

_____

_____

_____

POSTNUPTIAL AGREEMENTS

_____

_____

_____

_____

_____

_____

YOUR IRA AND/OR COMPANY PLAN BENEFICIARY FORMS

_____

_____

_____

_____

_____

_____

IRA CUSTODIAL AGREEMENTS (OR COMPANY RETIREMENT PLAN DOCUMENTS)

_____

_____

_____

_____

To create the most effective and useful plan, you must be prepared to share with your professional advisors (financial, legal, tax) all the personal and financial data you gathered in Part II. They will most certainly ask you for this, and they love it when you come prepared. It saves them so much time and saves you lots of money. It also shows them that you are serious about your short- and long-term financial goals, keeping your wealth away from the tax collector, and planning for your retirement and legacy.

Be prepared with this information so you don't blow the third act!

Part III

THE WINNING HALF
OF THE GAME

YOUR "EXIT PLAN" FOR PRESERVING YOUR WEALTH

I have left some space after each of the items in this section for you to jot down your own thoughts or action to take.

• **It's the score at the end of the game that counts!** It's not how much you make, it's how much you keep at the end of the game . . . when it counts . . . and how much of it is *tax free*.

• **Take it with you when you leave your employer or retire.** Do not leave your money with your employer, because 401(k) plans have fees (even if they say they don't), and your employer is not accountable to you. This is the time to move your 401(k), 403(b), 457, or other company retirement plan and work with your own financial planner.

• **Check your withdrawal options.** When leaving an employer or when retiring, you are better off doing an IRA rollover and taking total control of your money. Once the funds are in your own IRA, you have better investment and estate planning options. Also, you can guarantee the "stretch IRA" (that great parlay of wealth) for your loved ones. But if you have highly appreciated company stock in your company plan (this is called *net unrealized appreciation,* or NUA), or if you qualify for special ten-year averaging rates, it may be better for you to take a lump-sum distribution.

• **You potentially have a *big* tax problem when you withdraw at retirement.** I call it the "retirement savings time bomb." If your tax-deferred savings are a large part of your total assets, then your problem is bigger, since it will be these assets that will have to be withdrawn after your death to pay any applicable estate taxes, income taxes, and post-death expenses. This will result in a tax-on-tax scenario that instantly eats away at your retirement savings. Thanks to recently increased federal estate tax exemptions, many estates will be free of federal estate tax, but always check with your advisor.

• **Turn taxable money (e.g., your tax-deferred savings) into many times that amount and make it tax free, using the three biggest benefits in the U.S. Tax Code:**

1. *The tax exemption for life insurance.* You get great leverage, since you can use a relatively small amount of taxable money now to have your family end up with many times that amount, tax free.

Plus, you have *more money for you right now,* since you have already provided for your loved ones.

2. *The estate tax exemption.* You can use this only if you leave property, such as your retirement account or accounts, to someone other than your spouse—your children or grandchildren, for example. And if you don't use it, you lose it. Each spouse receives his or her own estate exemption. For 2009, the federal estate exemption is $3.5 million per person, so that would mean $7 million for a married couple. This will exempt many more estates from federal estate tax, but laws change, and you need to be aware that your plan will take into account whatever the *current* federal estate tax exemption is.

3. *The "stretch IRA."* The way your family can keep building upon your accumulated wealth is to make the government wait so long for its money that it can never catch up. This is what the "stretch IRA" does. Using the "stretch IRA," you can pass your IRA to your loved ones and they can take minimum distributions over the rest of their lives, giving only crumbs to the government each year while the accounts build for them, tax deferred.

• **A "stretch Roth IRA" is as good as it gets for your family.** If you pass a Roth IRA under your federal estate exemption, the distributions are not only income tax free, but estate tax free, too. This means that your family receives totally tax-free money *for life.*

• **It's not in your will.** The option to "stretch" should be automatic, but many families miss out if they do not have a proper and current IRA *beneficiary designation form,* or if they cannot find it when they need it—because retirement accounts should pass *outside the will.*

ITEMS I WANT TO KNOW MORE ABOUT:

_____

_____

_____

_____

PROBLEM AREAS:

_____

_____

_____

_____

ACTION I SHOULD TAKE:

_____

_____

_____

_____

_____

_____

_____

_____

_____

_____

_____

YOUR PLAN PROTECTION TIMELINE

This is an advance notification program to alert you to future events, deadlines, decisions, and opportunities in order to remove any uncertainty about the future of your plan and eliminate any costly mistakes before they can happen.

Life Events

These are perennial items that have no set date. The timing on these events is different for everyone.

Birth, death, marriage, divorce

- Update beneficiary forms

Milestone Ages for Distributions from Retirement Plans

Age Fifty

Plan exception to 10 percent penalty for public safety employees:

- If you are separated from service from your government-defined benefit pension plan in the year you turn age fifty or older and you are a public safety employee such as police, fire, or emergency medical worker, you can withdraw from the plan without paying the 10 percent penalty for early withdrawals. You nevertheless pay the income tax on any amounts withdrawn. This exception from the 10 percent early withdrawal penalty is available only for distributions from these government plans and not from other company plans or IRAs.

Age Fifty-five

Plan exception to 10 percent penalty:

- If you are separated from service from your company plan in the year you turn age fifty-five or older, you can withdraw from the plan without paying the 10 percent penalty for early withdrawals. You nevertheless pay the income tax on any amounts withdrawn. This exception from the 10 percent early withdrawal penalty is available only for distributions from company plans and *not* from IRAs.

Age 59½

All withdrawals from any kind of retirement plan or IRA are exempt from the 10 percent early withdrawal penalty once you reach age 59½. Distributions are still subject to regular income tax, however.

Age 70½

Required minimum distributions (RMDs) must begin from your IRA and from most company plans:

- Required minimum distributions must begin by your required beginning date, which is April 1 of the year following the year you turn age 70½.

- Exception for company plans only: If you are still working for your company past age 70½, you can delay your required beginning date from your company plan (if your plan allows this) until April 1 of the year following the year you retire. This exception applies only to company plans of companies that you do not own more than 5 percent of. It does not apply to the plan of your self-employed business, and it does not apply to IRAs.

Age Seventy-five

The 403(b) exception to the required beginning date age:

- If you have a 403(b) plan (generally for nonprofit or government employees such as teachers and hospital employees), and you had a balance in your plan as of December 31, 1986, you can delay distributions on that balance until you reach age seventy-five. This applies only to the balance as of December 31, 1986, not to the rest of your plan balance or to any other company plan or IRA.

1936

You must have been born before 1936 to qualify for the special ten-year-averaging tax break on a lump-sum distribution from your company plan. This break also applies to your beneficiaries of any age.

Distribution Confirmation

Whenever funds are withdrawn or transferred from one retirement account to another, make sure that you check that the funds were transferred or rolled over to the correct account.

- It is common for banks and financial institutions to transfer funds to the wrong account (e.g., a non-IRA account instead of the IRA where the funds were supposed to go). This could cause the amount withdrawn to be subject to an unintended tax and possibly a penalty if you are under age 59½.

- Even though you have sixty days to complete a rollover, check within thirty days (or sooner) to make sure the distribution is being made correctly; then check the very next statement to make sure the funds arrived where they were supposed to.

Dates and Events to Be Aware of During the Year

The items you will see here should have been addressed already, but this gives you a review of what to do when. It also serves as a final check on the most important items to take care of and the deadlines for each.

March

- Make sure your first required minimum distribution (RMD) is taken if you turned age 70½ in the prior year and did not yet take your RMD. It is due by April 1, but this should be checked now, in March.

April

- April 1 is the required beginning date for IRAs and plans where you turned age 70½ in the prior year.

- April 15 is the due date for tax returns (unless there is a valid extension on file).

- Automatic six-month extension to October 15 for everyone: April 15 is the last day to make IRA or Roth IRA contributions for the prior year. There is no extension on this, even if your tax return is on extension.

- SEP (simplified employee pension) contributions can be made up to the extended due date.

October

- October 15 is the last day to file taxes.

- October 15 is the last day to recharacterize Roth IRA conversions or contributions for the prior tax year.

- October 15 is the last day to remove prior year excess IRA contributions, plus or minus earnings, and handle all reporting on the tax return.

- The IRA trust deadline is October 31. This is only for your beneficiaries and only if you named a trust as your IRA beneficiary. If that is the case, a copy of the trust should be given to the IRA custodian by October 31 of the year following the year of the IRA owner's death in order to preserve the "stretch IRA" to your individual trust beneficiaries.

FOLLOWING UP ON AND KEEPING YOUR INFORMATION CURRENT

Do not ignore any of these items. *I put them all on this list because they are all important.* Not checking any one of these items could result in irreversible and expensive problems for either you or your loved ones.

I left space after each of these items for your own comments or questions.

1. Are your beneficiary forms current? Do they take into account life events that would change your choice of beneficiary (birth, death, marriage, divorce, beneficiaries to eliminate, marriage of children or grandchildren, adopted children, special needs, trusts)?

Changes in Beneficiaries:

PRIMARY

_____

_____

_____

_____

CONTINGENT

_____

_____

_____

_____

COMMENTS OR QUESTIONS TO FOLLOW UP ON:

_____

_____

_____

_____

2. Have you considered the effect of disclaimers in your planning?

A disclaimer is a right to refuse the inheritance so that your retirement account will pass to your next named beneficiary, your contingent beneficiary. (Naming contingent beneficiaries is the key to using this strategy.)

This is a very effective strategy that allows your beneficiaries more flexibility when they inherit.

COMMENTS OR QUESTIONS TO FOLLOW UP ON:

_____

_____

_____

_____

_____

_____

_____

3. Do your financial, legal, and/or tax advisors have up-to-date copies of all changed beneficiary forms?

COMMENTS OR QUESTIONS TO FOLLOW UP ON:

_____

_____

_____

_____

_____

_____

_____

_____

_____

4. Is your current beneficiary form the one that is on file with the financial institution?

You should have it *acknowledged* by the financial institution that it is the one on file.

COMMENTS OR QUESTIONS TO FOLLOW UP ON:

_____

_____

_____

_____

_____

_____

_____

_____

_____

5. Is your financial, legal, and/or tax advisor familiar with all of the distribution options permitted by your custodial agreements?

COMMENTS OR QUESTIONS TO FOLLOW UP ON:

_____

_____

_____

_____

_____

_____

_____

_____

_____

_____

6. Does your choice of beneficiary consider your overall estate plan and other assets?

What would the estate tax effect be of your choice of beneficiary?

Would you be better off not naming your spouse and instead naming children or grandchildren?

COMMENTS OR QUESTIONS TO FOLLOW UP ON:

_____

_____

_____

_____

_____

_____

_____

_____

7. Does your beneficiary form name a person (as opposed to your estate, a charity, or a trust)?

COMMENTS OR QUESTIONS TO FOLLOW UP ON:

_____

_____

_____

_____

_____

_____

_____

_____

_____

_____

8. If you will be naming a trust as your company plan or IRA beneficiary, are your attorney and advisor up to the task?

COMMENTS OR QUESTIONS TO FOLLOW UP ON:

_____

_____

_____

_____

_____

_____

_____

_____

_____

_____

9. Have you made any changes in multiple beneficiaries?

Make it clear what each new primary and contingent beneficiary's share is.

Make sure there is a fraction, a percentage, or the
word "equally" or "in equal shares," if that applies.

You may need to create separate accounts for each
new beneficiary or rely on beneficiaries to split their
inherited accounts in a timely way after they inherit.

COMMENTS OR QUESTIONS TO FOLLOW UP ON:

_____

_____

_____

_____

_____

_____

_____

10. Does your current beneficiary form allow a per stirpes option, so that if your beneficiary dies before you, that beneficiary's share will go to his or her children and not to someone else?

COMMENTS OR QUESTIONS TO FOLLOW UP ON:

_____

_____

_____

_____

_____

_____

_____

_____

_____

11. Will your custodial agreement with the financial institution allow the "stretch IRA" option for your family? Even though the law allows this, your institution does not have to. This is a critical point.

COMMENTS OR QUESTIONS TO FOLLOW UP ON:

_____

_____

_____

_____

_____

_____

_____

_____

_____

12. Will your custodial agreement allow your beneficiaries to name beneficiaries when they inherit?
(The beneficiary's beneficiary is called the *succes-
sor beneficiary.*)

COMMENTS OR QUESTIONS TO FOLLOW UP ON:

_____

_____

_____

_____

_____

_____

_____

_____

_____

13. Make sure that the funds your nonspouse beneficiaries inherit from you will not be held hostage by the financial institution.

Your custodial agreement should allow beneficiaries to move inherited funds by doing a trustee-to-trustee transfer. If not, your beneficiaries will be stuck at this financial institution or be forced to pay a huge tax to get their money out.

If the institution does not allow this option, then move your funds now to an institution that offers this option. Your beneficiaries will not have the leverage to do so.

COMMENTS OR QUESTIONS TO FOLLOW UP ON:

_____

_____

_____

_____

_____

_____

14. Will your custodial agreement accept a trust as your IRA beneficiary and pay annual required minimum distributions to that trust?

COMMENTS OR QUESTIONS TO FOLLOW UP ON:

_____

_____

_____

_____

_____

_____

_____

_____

_____

_____

15. Will your custodial agreement accept your power of attorney?

You need to know that *now,* not when you are ill or incompetent and need help with your plan transactions.

COMMENTS OR QUESTIONS TO FOLLOW UP ON:

_____

_____

_____

_____

_____

_____

_____

_____

16. Does the default provision in your custodial agreement tell who will inherit if there is no current beneficiary form on file with the institution, or if no one in your family can find it upon your death?

Your estate may be the default beneficiary, which will cause the loss of the "stretch IRA" for your family.

Inheritance Instructions for Your Family

Once your loved ones inherit, they will need guidance. The following are just some of the items your beneficiaries will need help with. Now is the time to have them meet with your advisors so there are no surprises that could foil your well-thought-out planning:

- Correct handling of the required distribution for the year of death

- Inherited IRA account titling (so that the funds are not immediately taxed and can be stretched over their lifetimes)

- Splitting IRAs after inheriting (for multiple beneficiaries)

- Required minimum distributions (which apply to your beneficiaries, too)

- Beneficiaries naming their own beneficiaries (i.e., who will inherit if they die early)

- Dealing with life insurance proceeds

- IRA trust management

- Changing investments on inherited IRAs (which can be moved only by doing trustee-to-trustee transfers, also known as *direct rollovers* or *direct transfers*)

_____

_____

_____

_____

_____

_____

_____

_____

COMMENTS OR QUESTIONS TO FOLLOW UP ON:

_____

_____

_____

_____

_____

_____

_____

_____

_____

_____

_____

Appendix

TEN FINANCIAL DISASTERS YOU CAN AVOID

You will find that this brings home many key points that should help enhance your understanding of the importance of investment and retirement planning and the items that need to be addressed.

Make notes of items that you want to know more about, problem areas you spot, or action you need to take.

1. Your Company Plan Savings and/or IRA Are Not Covered in Your Will

- Then you have no plan—no exit strategy—no one took care of this.

NOTES:

_____

_____

_____

_____

_____

2. Not Naming a Beneficiary for Your Company Plan or IRA Savings

- You need to name both primary and contingent beneficiaries.

- The beneficiary form determines the ultimate potential value of the account and trumps all other legal documents; in fact, it is the estate plan for what may be your largest single asset.

- Could cause probate.

- Lose "stretch IRA" (no designated beneficiary).

- Not keeping company plan or IRA beneficiary forms up to date.

NOTES:

_____

_____

_____

_____

_____

_____

3. Not Being Aware of Key Employer Change or Retirement Options

Not knowing how to decide whether you should:

- Roll over to an IRA

- Leave it in the plan or move to a new plan

- Take the money out and take advantage of the lump-sum distribution options

NOTES:

_____

_____

_____

_____

_____

_____

4. Costly Rollover Mistakes

You have one chance to do it right:

- Rollover versus trustee-to-trustee transfer

- Sixty-day rule

- Once per year rollover limit for IRAs

- 20 percent mandatory withholding from distributions from company plans

NOTES:

_____

_____

_____

_____

_____

_____

_____

5. Not Knowing about the "Stretch IRA" Option

NOTES:

_____

_____

_____

_____

6. Mistakes in Setting Up Inherited Accounts

These mistakes trigger immediate taxation of the entire inherited account:

- The "stretch IRA" option will be lost forever.

- The beneficiaries will receive a big tax bill.

These mistakes cannot be fixed:

- Titling mistakes are irreversible.

- Not knowing that a nonspouse beneficiary cannot do a rollover (only a spouse can do a rollover) is costly, taxwise. Most inherited accounts are wiped out because of this error.

- Do not put an inherited IRA in the beneficiary's *own* IRA.

- Do not move inherited funds—this should be done only by a trustee-to-trustee transfer.

Remember to have beneficiaries split inherited IRAs in a timely manner after death when there are multiple beneficiaries.

_____

_____

_____

_____

7. Missing the NUA Tax Break

The tax break for net unrealized appreciation (NUA) is often lost forever.

Advisors and financial institutions are often too quick to push the IRA rollover. Ask about highly appreciated company stock before doing the IRA rollover.

Do you have company stock in your 401(k) plan? If yes, then this applies to you!

_____

_____

_____

8. Not Being Aware of the Biggest Tax Break for Your Beneficiaries

It is the *income in respect of a decedent* (IRD) deduction.

This is often a very large tax deduction and is missed even by experienced CPAs.

NOTES:

_____

_____

_____

_____

9. Incorrect Use of Trusts as Beneficiaries

Trusts are not for everyone:

• There's no tax benefit.

• There can be severe tax problems if the trust does not meet special IRS requirements (and most don't).

• Trusts could accelerate taxes at high trust tax rates.

NOTES:

_____

_____

_____

_____

10. Advisor Loyalty—Sticking with the Wrong Advisor

Normally, loyalty is a very good quality, but your first loyalty is to yourself and your loved ones.

The worst mistakes are made right under the advisor's nose and often with his or her direct consent.

ITEMS I WANT TO KNOW MORE ABOUT:

_____

_____

_____

_____

PROBLEM AREAS:

_____

_____

_____

_____

_____

ACTION I SHOULD TAKE:

_____

_____

_____

_____

_____

No More Excuses: Get It Done

I have heard all the excuses and related horror stories.

Write down every excuse you can think of to avoid this planning . . . and then address each one so you can move on.

EXCUSES I HAVE USED TO PUT THIS PLANNING OFF FOR ANOTHER DAY:

_____

_____

_____

_____

_____

_____

_____

_____

Do You Want the Government Plan or Your Plan?
Get It Done Now!

When you create your own plan:

You have *more* money for you now

***More* for your retirement**

***More* for your loved ones**

. . . and *more* of it tax free!

More, more, more, more.

All the best to you!

—ED SLOTT

ABOUT THE AUTHOR

ED SLOTT is a nationally recognized retirement account tax expert and a professional speaker at conferences nationwide. He hosts www.irahelp.com, which provides retirement resources for both consumers and professional advisors. He created Ed Slott's Elite IRA Advisor Group,™ an exclusive registry of financial advisors. Slott is the author of *Your Complete Retirement Planning Road Map, Parlay Your IRA into a Family Fortune,* and *The Retirement Savings Time Bomb . . . and How to Defuse It.* He publishes *Ed Slott's IRA Advisor,* a monthly newsletter for financial professionals. He is a contributor to such publications as *The New York Times, The Washington Post, The Wall Street Journal, Time, Newsweek, Fortune, Forbes, Money,* and *USA Today,* and has been a frequent guest on national television. He lives on Long Island, New York.